THE TENT WITHOUT TILLY

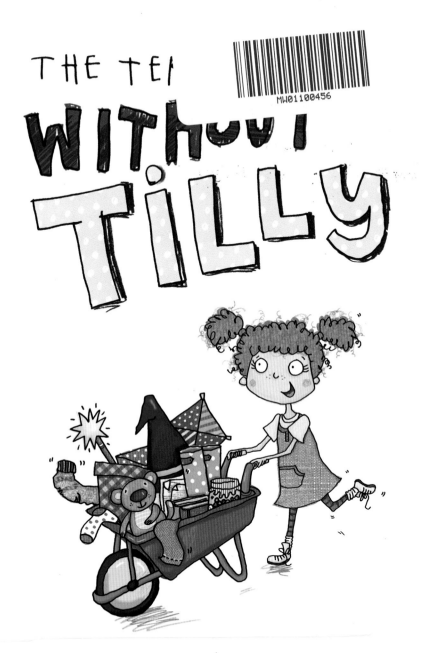

HILARY McKAY

ILLUSTRATED BY KIMBERLEY SCOTT

To Jim and Bella,
Whose bedrooms are beyond words.
With love from Mum
H.M.

for Stella and Bailey
K.S.

EGMONT
We bring stories to life

Book Band: Gold

First published in Great Britain 2012
This Reading Ladder edition published 2016
by Egmont UK Limited
The Yellow Building, 1 Nicholas Road, London W11 4AN
Text copyright © Hilary McKay 2012
Illustrations copyright © Kimberley Scott 2012
The author and illustrator have asserted their moral rights
ISBN 978 0 6035 7357 6
www.egmont.co.uk
A CIP catalogue record for this title is available from the British Library.
Printed in Malaysia
67760/1

Series consultant: Nikki Gamble

CONTENTS

Tilly (me!)

Granny

Uncle Kevin

The Rough Twins

Great Uncle Max

Reading Ladder

Mum & Dad

Timmy

♥ Polar

Granny

The Rough Lot

Uncle Kevin

The Rough Twins

Great Uncle Max

Tilly (me!)

TILLY AT HOME

Tilly, who had red hair and lots of good ideas, lived with:

Her father (who was a maths teacher).

Her mother (who was planning to write a book).

Her little brother Timmy (who was always good).

And Polar, her snow white dog.

They were a very happy family. Their house had hardly any spiders and they often had meals of lovely curry.

Tilly was a helpful girl.

She helped the dog into the bath.

She helped her mother cook the curry.

She helped her father mark his books.

She helped her brother learn to grow.

And if anyone needed help with their painting . . .

Or skating . . .

Or climbing . . .

Or digging . . .

Or their hosepipes or bikes or anything like that, Tilly was always ready.

'I like helping,' said Tilly.

Tilly had so many things she liked to do, that she never had time to do the things she didn't.

The thing that Tilly didn't like doing most of all was tidying her bedroom.

So she didn't.

Never ever.

'I haven't got time,' said Tilly.

This is what anyone saw who looked in the door of Tilly's bedroom:

Socks, jeans, crumby plates.

Crisp bags and chewed brown apple cores.

Shoes, wellies, chopped up paper, letters home from school.

Old balloons. Kites.

Shoe boxes, music boxes, lunch boxes, tipped-over boxes.

Dressing-up clothes.

Fourteen bears, four rabbits, two tigers, one elephant, three raggy dolls and one baby Annabel (not in her cot).

A sprinkle of school uniform.

Marbles.

Beads.

Dust.

Tilly's family could not bear Tilly's awful bedroom. They said: 'Tilly! Tidy up this room at once!'

'I will,' promised Tilly, 'as soon as I have time.'

But she didn't.

So then her family said:

'This mess is IMPOSSIBLE! We cannot put up with it ANY MORE!'

'If that is true,' said Tilly, 'I'm afraid I will have to go.'

So Tilly went into the garden.

Collected the big wheelbarrow.

Dragged it up the stairs.

Loaded it with her stuff.

Hugged everyone goodbye.

Said, 'I hope you can manage without me.'

And left.

At the corner of the road she turned back for one last look. Already she could hear the dragon-roar of the vacuum cleaner. From her open bedroom window poured clouds of grey dust.

When she waved to say goodbye, only three black bin bags waved back.

'Oh well,' said Tilly cheerfully. 'I shall go and see my dear old Granny.'

So off she went with the wheelbarrow to dear old Granny's house.

Granny

DEAR OLD GRANNY

When dear old Granny saw Tilly coming she
screamed with joy.

'Tilly darling!' she exclaimed. 'How long can
you stay?'

'For as long as my family can manage without
me,' said Tilly. 'If that's all right.'

'It's the nicest thing I can think of!' exclaimed
Granny, dancing about so that her pink beads
swung in loops round her neck. 'Come inside
at once!'

Granny's house was very pretty. All the walls
were pale pink. All the floors were rose red.

15

Granny helped Tilly carry her wheelbarrow up the stairs to the pinkest, tidiest bedroom that Tilly had ever seen.

'There!' said Granny. 'Just you unpack and get comfy, and then come down for tea.'

'Thank you, Granny,' said Tilly, upending the wheelbarrow all over the rosy carpet. 'I'll come right now. Already it looks like home.'

'Perfect,' said Granny, and she hurried downstairs to get tea.

Tea was raspberry buns, pink jelly and fairy cakes, all eaten at the little round table in Granny's bright kitchen.

'I'm so glad you're here,' said Granny, pouring glasses of strawberry milkshake. 'I do hope, Tilly, that you are not afraid of spiders?'

'Not a bit,' said Tilly. 'I always pop them outside when I find them at home.'

'What wonderful news,' said Granny. 'You can see, my dear, the terrible state I'm in.'

Tilly looked around.

At the delicious food.

At the flowers in the window.

At Granny's rosy face and shining silver hair.

'I think everything looks lovely!' she said in surprise.

'Darling,' said Granny. 'You haven't looked up.'

'Looked up?'

'At the ceiling,' whispered Granny.

'Oh,' said Tilly, and then she said,

'OH!'

19

There were big, quiet grey spiders, and long-legged danglers. Jet black staring ones like small, cross stars. Zigzagging darting ones, saggy baggy sulking ones, hairy ones that pounced.

'Would you like me to pop them outside?' asked Tilly helpfully.

'Oh, Tilly!' begged Granny. 'Do you think you possibly could?'

'Yes of course,' said Tilly, and she did.

The kitchen spiders.

The sitting room spiders.

The bathroom, landing and bedroom spiders.

20

Tilly balanced on chairs and climbed on tables and swung from curtains to reach the ceiling . . .

And she popped them all outside.

It was very late before the last spider was

gone and she tumbled into her little pink bed.

She did not wake up until Granny came tiptoeing into the room.

One of Granny's hands was hidden behind her back holding a large red envelope.

The other held the spider-catching jar.

'Tilly,' said Granny, 'all the spiders have gone to live in the shed! They came tumbling out in heaps when I opened the door! It would be so helpful, darling, if you would just . . .'

But Tilly thought she had been helpful

enough with Granny's spiders. So she loaded all her things back on to the wheelbarrow and bumped it down the stairs and into the garden.

'Thank you for the lovely tea,' she said, kissing Granny. 'The poor spiders must have somewhere to live. I'll visit once a week and take away any that have wandered back into the house, but now I really must go!'

So Granny kissed her back, tucked the large red envelope amongst the other things in the wheelbarrow, called 'No visitors!' very firmly in the direction of the shed, and hurried back into the house.

At the corner of the road Tilly turned to wave. Granny's door was tight shut, but a thousand spidery legs waved back from the shed.

'I shall visit Uncle Kevin,' decided Tilly, and she turned her wheelbarrow towards the distant towers of Uncle Kevin's house.

Uncle Kevin

UNCLE KEVIN'S HOUSE

Uncle Kevin's house looked lovely, with its flags and turrets and white swans swimming in the moat.

'Tilly, my dear!' called Uncle Kevin, and a minute later the drawbridge came rattling down and he hurried across to meet her.

'Tilly! How splendid!' he cried. 'Can you possibly stay for lunch?'

'Unless my family find they can't manage without me, I can stay for ages!' Tilly told him.

25

'Then come inside at once!'
said Uncle Kevin, and led the way
through the huge oak doors.

'Now where shall I put you?'
he asked. 'Bedroom? Billiard
room? Ballroom? Strong room?
Sitting room? Any of the state
rooms? What about the library?
What do you think?'

'I'd love the library,' said
Tilly.

'Then come this way!' said
Uncle Kevin, and led Tilly to the
most beautiful room she had ever
seen. It had large log fires burning
in the fire places at each end and
a wonderful swinging hammock
hung between two piles of books.

'Now, do make yourself at

home!' said Uncle Kevin, piling cushions into the hammock.

'Thank you,' said Tilly, and she tipped up the wheelbarrow so that things went skating to every corner of the polished floor. 'Did you mention lunch, Uncle Kevin?'

'I did, I did, I certainly did,' said Uncle Kevin, stepping round a lot of Lego and some mouldy conkers and things. 'I was thinking of curry,' he added, opening the door for Tilly. 'Curry, curry, curry, that's what I was thinking of! Come along to the kitchen and we will see what we can do!'

Uncle Kevin's kitchen was as big as a church. On a table in the middle stood a loaf of sliced bread, a buttery knife and a jar of Best Red Jam.

Uncle Kevin turned hopefully to Tilly.

'Curry would be wonderful,' he said, 'if only one knew where to begin!'

'Spices? Ginger? Onions?' suggested Tilly helpfully. 'Tomatoes? Chilli? Rice?'

Joyfully, Uncle Kevin swept the bread and jam off the table and began rushing around opening cupboards.

'Limes and coconuts? Red and green peppers?' said Tilly.

More and more ingredients began to be piled on to the table.

'Salt and saffron,' ordered Tilly, chopping busily. 'Oil and . . . Oy! Mind your fingers, Uncle Kevin!'

Uncle Kevin snatched his fingers from the chopping board just in time.

'I shall leave everything to you!' he told Tilly (sucking them). 'Clearly you are an expert!'

So Tilly roasted and simmered and stirred all afternoon. She had a lovely time. Uncle Kevin did not interfere at all, except to shout now and then, 'Hotter, my dear!'

Once Tilly heard a splash from the moat.

'Nothing to worry about!' called Uncle Kevin. 'Message in a bottle! Get 'em all the time!'

It was nearly dark before Tilly gave all of her saucepans one final stir.

'Lunch, Uncle Kevin!' she called at last.

'Hurrah!' cried Uncle Kevin, rushing into the kitchen. 'I've been thinking of curry,' he told Tilly, 'for years and years and years!'

That night, when Tilly climbed into her hammock she was very tired indeed. It seemed only a moment later that the library door was flung open.

'Good morning! Good morning!' cried Uncle Kevin. 'Don't be late for breakfast!'

'Breakfast?' asked Tilly.

'I thought *curry*!' said Uncle Kevin, so Tilly loaded up her wheelbarrow, and thanked him for the lovely hammock.

'Must you go?' asked Uncle Kevin sadly, as he pushed the message in a bottle into the corner of her wheelbarrow.

'I'm afraid I must,' said Tilly. 'But if you like I will come back next week and teach you to cook.'

'Me? Cook?' exclaimed

Toodle pip!

Uncle Kevin. 'No thank you, Tilly! How very jolly undignified that would be!'

And when Tilly looked back to wave from the drawbridge he had already turned away.

'There's nothing at all wrong with jam sandwiches!' he called over his shoulder as he vanished.

'Oh, well!' said Tilly. 'I shall visit the Rough Lot! That's what I'll do!'

The Rough Twins

THE ROUGH LOT

The Rough Lot were a large family who lived in a wild and crowded house. Tilly's dog had come from there, when he was a little snow white puppy.

When Tilly arrived, the father Rough Lot was adding up his bills and trying to work out if they mattered.

The mother Rough Lot was shouting at the three black Rough Lot dogs.

The Big Boys (and the dogs) were digging for treasure in the garden.

The twin toddler Rough Lots were fighting on the floor.

But they all stopped what they were doing to hug their cousin Tilly.

'How long can you stay?' they asked. 'Are you good at sums? Are you good at finding things? Are you good at washing dogs, and are you good at toddlers?'

Tilly hugged her cousins back, explained that she could stay for as long as her family could manage without her, and began being helpful at once.

That morning she:

1. Added up the bills (and proved they didn't matter).

2. Washed the black dogs white again.

3. Showed the Big Boys where to dig.

4. Tamed the toddlers so beautifully that they went hand in hand to bed for naps.

All the time that Tilly was busy the telephone rang. Each time, one of the Rough Lot grabbed it, said, 'Yes, yes! No, no!' and scribbled a rough note on a bit of rough paper. They stuffed the notes into Tilly's wheelbarrow (still unpacked until they found her anywhere to sleep).

'We will find somewhere,' they promised.
'As soon as we've shown you where the roof
needs mending.'

Tilly looked at the hole, decided she had been helpful enough, and told the Rough Lot very nicely that she had to go.

Nobody waved as she turned at the corner with her wheelbarrow, but that was not surprising.

They were all on the roof, holding tight.

'Don't let go!' called Tilly, waving anyway, and then she set off to visit Great Uncle Max.

Great Uncle Max

GREAT UNCLE MAX

When Tilly arrived at Great Uncle Max's house he had just finished packing his hot air balloon for a trip round the world.

'Have you come to wave goodbye?' he asked Tilly.

'No, Great Uncle Max,' said Tilly. 'I'm tired of waving goodbye. Nobody ever waves back.'

'Then you had better come with me,' said Great Uncle Max kindly, and he helped Tilly and her wheelbarrow into the basket of the balloon and untied the rope that was holding them to the ground.

The balloon began to rise.

Very slowly.

Because of the weight of the wheelbarrow.

'I'm sorry it's so boring,' said Great Uncle Max. 'Perhaps you brought something to read?'

At first Tilly thought she hadn't. Then she remembered she had. The big red envelope, the message in the bottle and all the rough notes that the Rough Lot had written. So she said, 'Thank you, Great Uncle Max. I'm sure I won't be bored,' and settled down in a corner to read.

She read and read, and the basket rose higher.

'A surprising lot of messenger pigeons about today,' said Great Uncle Max. 'Clever the way they found you!'

42

43

'Mmm,' said Tilly, reading.

'Arrows, now!' said Great Uncle Max, a moment later. 'We're being fired at, Tilly!'

'Mmm,' said Tilly, still reading:

TILLY, TILLY, PLEASE COME HOME!

WE MISS YOU VERY MUCH!

... WHY YOU DID NOT HAVE TIME TO TIDY YOUR BEDROOM!

WE UNDERSTAND NOW ...

LOOK WHERE THE ARROWS ARE POINTING!

The arrows were the sort with suckers on the end. They stuck on the hot air balloon in the pattern of an arrow.

It pointed to an aeroplane, zigzagging through the sky.

'TILLY! LOOK!' cried Great Uncle Max, so at last Tilly stopped reading and looked.

A banner trailed behind the plane:

DARLING TILLY, THE HOUSE IS FULL OF SPIDERS, POLAR IS AS BLACK AS COAL AND DADDY CANNOT DO HIS SUMS. ALSO THE RECIPE FOR CURRY IS LOST AND YOUR LITTLE BROTHER TIMMY IS NO LONGER GOOD AT ALL, AND WE CANNOT MANAGE WITHOUT YOU ANY LONGER!

'Great Uncle Max!' cried Tilly. 'Please could I borrow a parachute?'

The waving and the cheers when Tilly came parachuting home!

The laughter and the bouncing and the tight, tight hugs!

Tilly's father made a banner:

HOME IS WHERE THEY NEED YOU MOST!

Tilly's mother wrote a book (very like the
one that you have nearly finished reading):
The Terrible Tidy Time Without Tilly.
The book contained a special message to
parents:

PARENTS!
DO NOT MAKE
YOUR CHILDREN
TIDY UP THEIR
TERRIBLE
BEDROOMS

THEY ARE SURE
TO HAVE
MANY
MORE IMPORTANT
THINGS TO DO!